P9-ECW-080

# *Sled Dogs*

# Sled Dogs

## Brigid Casey & Wendy Haugh

Illustrated with photographs, old prints, and diagrams

**DODD, MEAD & COMPANY**
**NEW YORK**

CHATTANOOGA - HAMILTON CO.
BICENTENNIAL LIBRARY

ResC
J636.73
Cas
cop.1

*To the men in our lives:*
*Dennis and Liam,*
*Chuck and Henry and Joshua*

*Illustrations courtesy of:* Abi-Hassoun, photos by Mike Kops, 6, 76; Alaska Historical Library, Lomer Bros. Collection, 40, 47, 48, 55 *top*; Alaska Historical Library, A. G. Simmer, photographer, 49; Alpo, 60; David W. Armstrong, Jr., 17, 31, 55 *bottom*; Erick L. Armstrong, 34 *bottom*; Barbara Brisgel, "Barbicon," Morristown, N.J., Callea Photo, 77; Brigid Casey, 18, 20 *top*, 57, 61, 67; John G. Christman, *title page*, 32, 63 *top*; Jack Clune, Scotia, N.Y., photos by Brigid Casey, 26 *left*, 58; Virginia Corcoran, Sedalia, Co., 20 *bottom*; Bill Crosby, 28, 33, 59, 62, 63 *bottom*; Lyndon W. Ellis, 34 *top*, 70; Jean Fournier, "Toko," Canton, Ct., and Angela Porpora, "Mirkwood," Croton Falls, N.Y., photograph by Richard K. LaBranche, 66; Margaret Garrick, Highland Kennels, Broadalbin, N.Y., photos by Brigid Casey, 22, 68 *left*; Wendy Haugh, 29, 30, 38, 69; Arthur J. Hughes, 74; Ted Lewin, 14, 26 *right*; Library of Congress, 45; Edgar and Ellen Morey, Go Kennels, Northville, N.Y., photos by Brigid Casey, 24, 39, 68 *right*; Schenectady *Gazette*, photos by Sid Brown, 72, 75; U.S. Army Signal Corps, 41, 51, 52; U.S. Navy, 43.

Copyright © 1983 by Brigid Casey-Meyer and Wendy Haugh
All rights reserved
No part of this book may be reproduced in any form
without permission in writing from the publisher
Distributed in Canada by McClelland and Stewart Limited, Toronto
Manufactured in the United States of America

1  2  3  4  5  6  7  8  9  10

Library of Congress Cataloging in Publication Data

Casey, Brigid.
  Sled dogs.

  Includes index.
  Summary: Discusses the evolution of dogs; sled dog breeds, particularly the Eskimo dog, Alaskan Malamute, the Samoyed, and the Siberian Husky, and their uses; and sled dog racing.
  1. Sled dogs—Juvenile literature. 2. Sled dog racing—Juvenile literature. [1. Sled dogs. 2. Sled dog racing] I. Haugh, Wendy. II. Title.
SF428.7.C37  1983      636.7'3      83-14134
ISBN 0-396-08225-4

# Contents

SEP 84

*Man's best friend. This is a young female Malamute.*

# 1 _____Origin of the Dog_

The earliest ancestor of the domestic dog was a small undoglike creature, *Miacis*, that climbed trees in the dense forests of fifty million years ago. From *Miacis* evolved *Hesperocyon*, a carnivorous creature with a long, weasel-like body and short legs. *Hesperocyon* bore little resemblance to the dog, yet possessed many doglike traits.

Twenty-five to thirty million years ago, two definitely doglike creatures, both descendants of *Hesperocyon*, appeared upon the open plains. One of these, *Temnocyon*, became ancestor to the present-day wild dogs of Africa, India, and Brazil. The other, *Cynodesmus*, is ancestor to an intermediate creature called *Tomarctus*. Modern-day wolves, jackals, coyotes, and foxes evolved from the wolf-like *Tomarctus*. It is the general feeling today that the wolf is the most immediate ancestor of the domestic dog.

Believe it or not, the dog has *not* always been "man's best friend." On the contrary, the caveman and the wild dog were fierce rivals in the primitive world, each hunting the same game in order to survive. The dog could easily outrun man. But man had arms, hands, fingers, and a sharp mind in his favor. He could fashion weapons, swing clubs, and hurl rocks, which enabled him to catch prey as well as defend himself against attacks by dogs.

The dogs soon learned that by following along on man's hunting trips—keeping well beyond arm's throw—they could feast upon those portions of the carcass that man did not eat on the spot or carry away to his cave. As time went on, man and dog entered into a hunting relationship. The dogs would chase and corner animals too fast moving for man to catch but too dangerous for the dogs to kill. Then man would move in with his weapons, taking what he wanted of the kill and leaving the rest for the dogs.

Wild dogs learned to hang around man's caves, where scraps of unwanted food were tossed aside. Both dog and man profited—the dog from the food, and man from the "clean-up" crew.

At some point, man undoubtedly discovered the dogs' dens and carried harmless puppies back to the caves. Unlike their wild parents, the pups grew up unafraid of humans. Generations passed, and more and more dogs were born into the ways of man—the cooperative rather than the competitive hunt; the sharing of food, warm fire, and comradeship.

As the dog's memories of roaming the wilderness in packs diminished, its loyalty to man increased, and the close bond of friendship between man and dog was established.

# 2 _____ *Sled Dog Breeds*

*The Eskimo Dog*

About 35,000 years ago, migrant tribes headed north into the Arctic regions with their dogs. These people, who came to be known as Inuits, or Eskimos, allowed their dogs to breed indiscriminately with Arctic wolves or other dogs. Over the years, through survival of the fittest, the Eskimo dogs developed certain characteristics that set them apart from other breeds. By about 3500 B.C., the feet, coats, heads, and tails of these Northern dogs had adapted to the harsh climate of their snowy world.

Eskimos, whether from Eastern Siberia, Alaska, the Canadian Arctic, or Greenland, lived a unique lifestyle for thousands of years. They needed a form of transportation geared to travel in snow, ice, and below-zero temperatures. No one is sure when the Eskimo decided to harness his ever present

*Old print from a Victorian geography was captioned "Life in the frigid zone." Note the sled and dogs.*

dog, but prehistoric drawings on bones and rocks depict Eskimo travel by dog sled in both North America and northern Russia well before 1000 B.C. Explorers have found ivory sled runners dating back as far as A.D. 1.

The Eskimo called his dog *Kingmik* and depended on his team for hunting as well as for travel. The dogs were often of no particular breeding but rather made up of many different strains. Although life without his dogs would have been much harder for an Eskimo, only a few tribes gave the animals more than minimal care. Often dogs were punished by severe beatings or by having their tails cut off. Some tribes kept puppies in total darkness until they were old enough to be put to work. This was done on the theory that the dogs would be so glad to get out into the light that they would run and run. Tribes that took good care of their dogs were very much in the minority.

Of necessity, Eskimo dogs became hardy, able to spend their whole lives in temperatures that often dropped to 60 or 70 degrees below zero. Their double-layered coats provided protection from the elements. The shaggy outer coat was long and coarse; the woolly undercoat was very dense and full of oils, which made it virtually waterproof.

To keep from slipping on the ice, Northern dogs had developed "snowshoe feet"—large and flat with a protective, cushioning growth of hair between the toes. Pads were thick and tough. Strong, short toenails helped grip the ice.

Arctic dogs had learned to carry their tails curled above their backs, thus preventing them from becoming hardened with frozen snow. Eventually this too became a genetic trait. The dogs used their tails to cover their noses when sleeping. This warmed the air as they breathed and prevented their lungs from freezing. Dogs that had been punished by having their tails cut off suffered from the cold.

As time passed, some Eskimos looked for dogs with bodies that were short, heavy boned, and muscular, with deep chests and well-sprung ribs. They preferred wedge-shaped heads that were well proportioned, with heavy muzzles and medium-sized eyes set obliquely into the head. Ears had to be

*Their double-layered coats allowed Eskimo dogs to work in temperatures of 48° below zero, as this team is doing in Canada.*

thick, triangular, alert, and well furred on the inside. The Eskimo was not particular about color. Any shade would do, but the dogs were usually brown, black, or gray. Eskimos chose dogs no taller than 25 inches at the shoulders so they would fit the harness straps. Weight varied from 50 to 85 or more pounds.

Eskimo dogs survived on diets of whatever was available —blubber, fish, bear, walrus skins, other dogs. It was not uncommon for the dogs to try to eat their own harnesses. Because they ran better on empty stomachs, the dogs were fed every other day when working. In the winter their meals were quite often frozen into solid blocks. Eating snow was the only way for them to quench their thirst.

A dog with a keen sense of smell was an invaluable aid to the Eskimo. Such dogs had the ability to sniff out a seal's breathing hole through layers of snow and ice, or scent a polar bear. It is interesting that the only animal the Eskimo dogs would not attack was the wolf. Perhaps this was because the Eskimo dog, despite its domestication, still howled like a wolf. The dogs were often tempted when the moon was full to lift their heads and join the nightly wolf chorus!

Usually one dog evolved as the leader of a team. Fights to the death for this position earned the Eskimo dogs the reputation of being mean and untrustworthy, but this was not necessarily true. With a little care and affection, Eskimo dogs could become fine pets. They were, when given a chance, obedient, intelligent, hard working, and alert. To live in such extreme weather conditions demanded nothing less.

Today, although the lifestyle of the Eskimo has changed considerably, the Eskimo dog is still very popular and in much demand for racing. Even though the American Kennel

*Eskimo dogs were muscular with heavy muzzles and alert ears.*

Club does not recognize the Eskimo dog at this time, there are many fanciers who feel it is indeed a pure breed rather than a conglomerate. The Canadian Kennel Club does recognize it as such and its requisites reflect the characteristics established when some of the Eskimos sought to standardize the breed. The Eskimo dog is pack oriented, a primitive dog rather than a pet in most cases.

The term "Eskimo dog," by the way, is often loosely and erroneously applied to any dog bearing similar characteristics. This is not correct, but the relationship between the Eskimo dog and other AKC-recognized Arctic breeds is indisputable.

### The Alaskan Malamute

The Alaskan Malamute is one of the three most popular breeds of Arctic sled dog recognized today by the AKC. Although, as with all Northern breeds, its origins are uncertain, the Malamute lays claim to being one of the oldest

*The standard for the Alaskan Malamute calls for a powerful dog with a deep chest, wide-set ears, and a plumelike tail.*

breeds of dog on record. Some historians feel it developed in Greenland, while others say perhaps Russia. The only certain fact is that Malamutes have been in Alaska for generations. Perhaps justly, Alaskans feel their state is the true homeland of the breed.

Malamutes were named after a tribe of Inuits called Mahlemuts. This tribe settled along the shores of upper western Alaska in the Kotzebue Sound area. The Mahlemuts were one of those few tribes of Eskimos that really cared for their dogs. They understood the importance of having exceptional dogs for transportation as well as for hunting. Early Russian and English explorers left written testimonies to this care. As a matter of fact, the Mahlemuts have not been mentioned in the early records without a reference to their superior dogs. Still other white men, arriving soon after the United States purchased Alaska in 1867, were impressed by the Mahlemut tribe and its dogs.

However, the dogs, in spite of the good care they received from their owners, found that life in the Northern regions was still harsh. They had to learn not only to exist but also to thrive on slim rations of often unappetizing food. To this day, Malamutes remain light eaters. The breed developed great strength and endurance as well as the ability to live outdoors in any climate. Teams could cover long distances at moderate speeds, often over terrain that seemed impassable.

As white men began to settle in Alaska, Malamutes began to breed with outside dogs. The period between 1909 and 1918 became known as the time of "decay of the Arctic sledge dog." It was during these gold-rush years that sled dog racing became very popular. Men tried many different breeding experiments in hopes of developing a winning team.

Fortunately for the Malamute, in the 1920's a couple who fancied the breed, Mr. and Mrs. Milton Seeley, devoted well over a year to straightening out its bloodlines. They actually lived in an Eskimo village and traced pedigrees. The AKC recognized the Malamute in the 1930's, basing the standard —the ideal—for the breed on the work of the Seeleys. Three studs were registered to start a pure line of foundation stock.

The standard calls for a powerful dog with a deep chest, a strong compact body, and a straight back. The Malamute must have the snowshoe feet of the Arctic dog, as well as the thick outer guard coat protecting the woolly undercoat. It must carry its tail over the back as if it were waving a plume.

The head of a Malamute must be broad and powerful, with a large bulky muzzle. Ears of medium size are set wide apart on the outside back edges of the skull. When erect, the ears must point slightly forward. Often when the dogs are working the ears are folded against the skull.

A slight furrow between brown, almond-shaped eyes marks the Malamute. The oblique positioning of the eyes gives this breed of dog a wolf-like appearance. However, the amiable expression in the eyes belies this.

Colors may range from light gray to black. White is the only solid color allowed. Underbodies and parts of legs and feet may have symmetrical white markings. Broken color extending over the body in spots or splashes is undesirable. On the face, white markings may resemble either a cap or a mask. Normally Malamutes are free from odor and only shed twice a year. Size may range from 23 to 25 inches at the shoulders and weight from 75 to 85 pounds, although larger and heavier dogs are now being bred.

As a result of the special relationship between the Mahlemut and his dog, the Alaskan Malamute is a family dog offering affection and faithfulness. It is a loyal, devoted companion and is good with children. Once they have reached maturity, Malamutes are well known for their dignified behavior and will only play when invited. Although gentle and trustworthy, Malamutes are also courageous and can be very fierce when necessary.

Besides their traditional roles of transportation and hunting, Malamutes have been used for other diversified jobs. They have been sent on many search and rescue missions, and have served at the front of both World Wars. They have gone on Arctic and Antarctic expeditions, performing exceptionally under the most adverse weather conditions. Unfortunately, after one of these expeditions, the dogs were

*Teeka, a sled dog of today, is half wolf, half Malamute.*

chained to an ice floe that was blown up. This event almost destroyed one of the three AKC lines and the registry had to be reopened to admit a new line.

Today, although they still are used occasionally for heavy hauling, Malamutes are bred primarily to be house pets or for the fun of racing or showing. The breed is a popular performer in the show ring and in the sport of obedience.

*The Samoyed*

The Samoyed (pronounced sam-uh-YEHD) is named after the nomadic people with whom it lived in Iran over one thousand years before Christ. Tribal warring in Iran forced the Samoyed tribe to move its families, herds of reindeer, and dogs northward through Mongolia. Eventually the Samoyed people settled on the endless tundra of northern Russia known today as Siberia.

Called *Bjelkier* by tribesmen (meaning white dog that

*As they did on the frozen Siberian tundras centuries ago, the Samoyeds in this team work hard for their driver.*

breeds white), the Samoyed served its masters for centuries as faithful sled dog, reindeer herder, home guard dog, and pet. The dog towed its master's boats and sledges and helped with the daily hunting and fishing. After working hard all day, the Samoyed was welcomed into the tribal hut at night, where it slept with its master, providing him with friendship and an indispensable source of heat. Over the centuries, this unusually close relationship between man and dog has endowed the Samoyed with a uniquely gentle and loving disposition, making it an ideal family dog.

The Samoyed, one of the oldest breeds of dog in existence, has changed little over the centuries. Its domestic, sheltered life protected it from much interbreeding with wolf or fox in the wild, and it is considered to be virtually a true breed.

An extremely strong dog, the Samoyed weighs between 35 and 60 pounds and is capable of pulling 1½ times its own weight. The male stands 21 to 23½ inches at the shoulders, the female 19 to 21.

Samoyeds are best known for their magnificent double coats, bleached light by generations of arctic sun and snow and ranging in color from pure white to beige to cream. The dog's soft inner coat insulates it from summer heat as well as winter cold. Combings from the Samoyed's coat can be spun and woven into fabric. Hairs from the woolly undercoat lend softness to the fabric, while the harsh outer hairs lend strength.

The Samoyed carries its heavily furred tail forward when at the alert. Its head is broad, with rounded and thickly furred ears, a medium muzzle, and a black nose. The eyes are dark and almond shaped.

ABOVE: *Because its lips curve, the Samoyed seems to smile, reflecting a cheerful disposition. The beautiful white coat is double.*

BELOW: *Riding the runners behind a flying 5-dog hitch of Samoyeds. Kira, on lead, is the dam of the others, 3½-year-old littermates.*

The "smile" that seems to radiate from the face of a Samoyed comes as a natural result of lips that curve slightly upward at the corners. This smile is a fitting symbol of the breed's cheerful and friendly personality.

The feet of the Samoyed are the large and flat snowshoe feet, with tough pads and protective hair tufts between the toes. The powerful hind legs give the breed a good rear-action drive.

Teams of Samoyeds were used by the Russians in the seventeenth and eighteenth centuries to chart the Siberian coast from the borders of Europe to the Bering Strait. Russian *Yassak* men, or tax collectors, even used Samoyed teams to gather taxes for the Czar.

In 1889, Ernest Kilburn-Scott, a member of England's Royal Zoological Society, brought the first Samoyed to England. He had purchased one male dog while on a Russian expedition. It was Kilburn-Scott who named the dogs in honor of their tribal masters. In 1896, Kilburn-Scott imported a female Samoyed from Russia to mate with his dog. From these two animals came the first litter of Samoyeds to be bred in England.

The breed was brought to the United States in 1904 by European royalty. Within ten years, the Samoyed had captured the fancy of several American breeders. By the end of World War I, forty Samoyeds were registered with the American Kennel Club. Fifteen of these had been imported from England, and three had come from the kennels of the Czar.

A handful of Samoyeds were released from Russia to other countries between 1889 and 1912, and about another half dozen in the 1920's. After the fall of the Czar, the Soviet

Union closed its doors and allowed no more of the beautiful white dogs to leave.

The Samoyed first gained worldwide acclaim as a sled dog in the polar expeditions of the late 1800's. Today, nearly all Samoyeds living outside of the Soviet Union are descendants of these expedition dogs.

*The Siberian Husky*

The Siberian Husky had its beginnings over three thousand years ago in the Kolyma River Basin of northeastern Siberia among an isolated tribe of people called the Chukchi. The Chukchi sled dogs, from which the present-day Siberian Husky descended, were valued not only as the tribe's single source of transportation but also as guards for the home and companions for the children. Like the Samoyed tribe, the Chukchi incorporated sled dogs into their family life, thereby helping to instill within their dogs a remarkably gentle nature.

*These Siberian puppies are descendants of the Chukchi sled dogs.*

Siberia's harsh climate greatly influenced the development of the Chukchi sled dog's physical characteristics. Since only the fittest dogs could survive the rigors of arctic living, weak traits were eliminated. The dog evolved into an animal of compact size with great speed, strength, and stamina. It was bred to pull light loads at moderate speeds over extremely long distances on very little food. The Chukchis' isolation from other tribes, coupled with their dedication to a highly selective and intelligent breeding system, enabled the Chukchi sled dog to remain a relatively pure and unchanged breed for thousands of years.

The last purebred Chukchi sled dogs vanished from Siberia during the 1930's as a result of the Soviet Union's large-scale program to standardize native tribes, traditions, and breeds of dogs. Fortunately, by this time, enough of the Chukchi sled dogs had been exported from the Soviet Union to insure the breed's continuation in other countries.

In the summer of 1908, a Russian fur trader named William Goosak brought the first team of Siberian Huskies, as the Chukchi sled dog came to be called in the States, to North America to compete in the 1909 All-Alaska Sweepstakes. The trader's team placed third in the second running of this difficult race.

Later that same year, impressed by the successful run, a Scotsman, Fox Maule Ramsay of Nome, chartered a schooner and crossed the Bering Sea to Siberia. There, he located a Chukchi village and returned to Alaska with seventy dogs. These dogs proved to be fine racing animals, competing against Alaska's best racing teams and winning. When Ramsay entered three teams in the 1910 All-Alaska Sweepstakes and placed first, second, and third, the breed gained popularity among Alaskan racing enthusiasts.

*Toot-ee-toot, an 11-year-old registered Siberian Husky, is from the old Leonhard Seppala line. She ran a single-dog lead for nine years, winning many races.*

A great sled dog driver, Leonhard Seppala, introduced the first team of Siberian Huskies to the conterminous United States in the 1920's. While in the States, he was invited to compete with his team in New England sled dog races.

Seppala's dogs were scorned as featherweight contenders by native New Englanders, whose large racing dogs averaged 100 pounds each in contrast to the Siberians' 50 to 55 pounds. Despite skepticism, Seppala's dogs proceeded to win each race that they entered.

When he returned to Alaska, Seppala left several Siberian Huskies in New England, where the breed flourished. As demand for the Siberians increased, more dogs were brought down from Alaska, and the beautiful, fast-moving, gentle-natured breed became firmly established in the States.

The male Siberian Husky generally stands 21 to 23½ inches at the shoulders and weighs 45 to 60 pounds. Somewhat smaller, the female stands 20 to 22 inches and weighs 35 to 50 pounds. Foxlike in appearance, light boned and fairly compact in body, the Siberian is considered to be one of the more fleet footed of the Arctic dogs.

The head of the Siberian Husky is relatively narrow, with strong jaws and high-set ears. Beautiful and unusual markings occur around the face and eyes. The eyes can be brown or light blue or one of each color.

The Siberian Husky has a double coat, yet lacks the coarse outercoat of the Alaskan Malamute and the Samoyed. Its undercoat is soft and downy, its outercoat thick yet smooth textured. The fur ranges in color from white and tan to wolf-gray, silver, and black. Like the Malamute, the Siberian Husky has no doggy odor, and surprisingly, it is not a source of irritation to people who suffer from allergic reactions to most breeds of dogs.

Most people think the Siberian Husky and the Alaskan Malamute resemble each other closely. But once the differences between them are learned, it is easy to tell the breeds apart.

One of the more obvious differences is eye color. As we have seen, the eyes of the Alaskan Malamute are always brown, while the Siberian Husky can have brown or blue eyes, or one of each color, according to AKC standards.

The ear set is different for each breed. The Siberian Husky's ears are set higher on the head, tips pointing straight up;

*Note the differences in eye and ear set between the Siberian Husky, left, and the Alaskan Malamute, right.*

the Malamute's ears are farther apart, slightly rounded at the top, and seem to stand off from the head.

Malamutes have heavier muzzles than the Siberians, and they carry their tails differently, waving them like a fan or a plume. The Siberian's tail flows straight out or slightly down when in motion. The Malamute's coat stands out from the body while the Siberian's coat falls more softly.

Alaskan Malamutes are generally larger and more powerful than the slighter Siberian Huskies. And, while not so obvious to the eye, Siberians are better at pulling lighter loads faster. Malamutes are better at hauling heavy loads over longer distances.

There are other purebred breeds that have been used for sledging in individual countries. Among these are the Great Pyrenees, the Newfoundland, and the Norwegian Elkhound.

26

# 3 _____ *The Dog in Harness*

*Dogs for Power*

The dog was the first animal to be domesticated by man, as well as one of the first animals to be harnessed for use as a draft, or working, animal. There is evidence that Mesolithic man (about 8000 B.C.) traveled on skis, with his dogs running freely at his side. Man had not yet thought of designing and building sleds to which a team of dogs could be hitched.

However, a major advancement was taking place: trade had begun. Seacoast civilizations discovered that inland communities wanted seashells for jewelry. The desire to trade led to the necessity for faster, more efficient means of transportation. About 7000 B.C., the first sled with runners originated in ice-covered northern Europe. Yet women, not dogs, were strapped to these first sleds by hide thongs—the men needed their arms free to ward off attackers.

*Two-year-old son of a purebred Samoyed and Siberian Husky/German Shepherd pulls cross-country skier as another pet frisks ahead. No one knows when the first dog pulled the first person on skis.*

Although it is uncertain exactly where and when dogs were first hitched to sleds, we do know that, through the years, different areas developed different sleds, all designed to be built and repaired easily out of existing materials. Flexibility was important so the sleds could survive the battering they received when crossing rough ice. Perhaps the two most popular types were the plank sled of Canada and Greenland and the frame sled of Alaska and Siberia.

The plank sled was light with two broad runners that

prevented it from sinking in soft snow. There were a series of crosspieces between the runners. Wood, whale jawbones, or frozen animal skins were used to make the plank sleds.

The Alaskan frame sled was a narrow, basket-shaped frame built on runners. It was always made of wood. Ash was favored, although oak, hickory, and birch were also used. These polar sleds were broad with narrow runners. They were used for traveling over hard, blue sea ice.

Different hitches were developed to attach the dogs to the sleds. The fan hitch was most often used with the plank sled. This type of harnessing connected all the dogs to the sled at one point. The dogs ran side by side in a fan formation. If a polar bear was sighted, all the dogs could be released at once to chase the bear and bring it to bay. This hitch was better for open, clear areas because it was so wide.

*Diagram of the fan hitch*

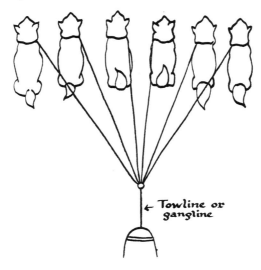

← Towline or gangline

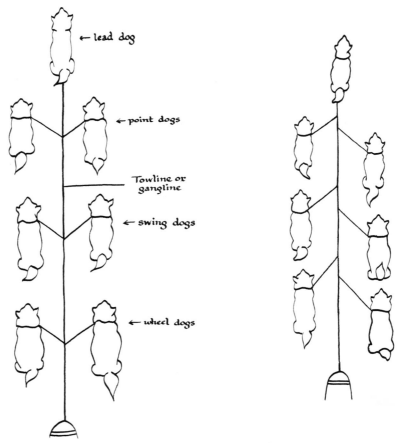

*Diagrams of the gang hitch, left, and the tandem hitch, right*

The dogs usually were attached to the frame sled in a gang hitch. This method harnessed the dogs in pairs along a central line called the gangline or towline.

Another form of hitch was the tandem, which placed dogs singly and alternately along the towline. Very narrow trails called for this formation. If one dog fell into a crevass, or off the trail, the tandem hitch prevented the unlucky animal from taking other dogs with it.

The basket of the sled held supplies. Passengers were only carried in emergencies. The driver ran or walked behind the sled. Sometimes the musher, as the driver was often called, rode on the runners and sometimes he "pedaled," keeping one foot on a runner while pushing the ground with his other foot. The action is similar to that required to ride a scooter or a skateboard. Skill is required to be a good pedaler. Each push must be synchronized with the overall movement of the team to avoid jerking the sled and throwing the dogs off stride.

*A modern racing sled, left, and a passenger sled. Today's racing sled developed from the old passenger sled.*

LEFT: *Five-dog team in gang hitch.* RIGHT: *Four-dog hitch with a double lead photographed from the Northville Bridge over the Great Sacandaga Lake, New York.*

Depending on the size of the team—anywhere from three to eight or more dogs—distances of more than forty miles could be traveled in one day. This far, while pulling loads of often more than double the team's collective weight!

The dogs were harnessed to the sleds by a series of lines usually made of rawhide. Unless the dogs were watched carefully, the Eskimo might go to hitch his team only to find the lines gone. As stated, the rawhide harness was almost irresistible to the hungry dogs.

The harness was fitted to each dog's body, allowing the strain and pressure of pulling to rest on the dog's shoulders and chest rather than its throat. If the dogs had been harnessed around their throats, as early work horses were, their pulling strength would have been cut in half. Harnessing around the animal's throat meant that the harder it pulled the more it choked itself. Fortunately, early-day dog owners realized this more quickly than did those who worked with horses, and they developed an appropriate harness. Freedom of the dog's legs and hindquarters was also necessary.

The gang and tandem hitches especially used neck and tug lines. The neck line went from the dog's collar to the towline. It held the dog in place and was useful in tying the dogs when they were at rest. Tug lines running from the harness across the dog's back to the towline helped lessen the stress on the neck.

### The Lead Dog

The strength of a good working team lay in its lead dog, then as it does today. The lead dog ran at the head of the

*A homemade sled and a pet dog add up to fun on a winter afternoon as the musher pushes off. Note the harness and how it is fitted to take the strain off the dog's neck.*

ABOVE: *Edgar Morey rides runners as Alaskan Husky single-leads another Alaskan Husky and Blue-tick Coonhound through Adirondack woods.*

BELOW: *David Armstrong, Jr.'s, team of Siberian/Malamute/wolf strains in a 9-dog, double-lead gang hitch, Montana.*

team, guided only by the oral commands of the driver. No reins were used by the musher while driving, only his voice. Since the rest of the dogs were trained to follow the leader, not the driver, it was crucial that the lead dog obey his master's every word. Therefore, the success of a team depended largely upon the ability of the lead dog and driver to work together effectively.

A good lead dog was intelligent, strong, fast, and obedient. The leader had to be able to outrun the majority of its peers, thereby maintaining tight lines between teammates. The lead dog had to know how to avoid collision while passing other teams on the trail.

A single lead dog was usual but, in cases of bigger teams, a double lead was often used. It was also standard practice to use the double lead when training a new lead dog. Having an extra dog ready to lead was a form of insurance.

A leader could be either male or female, as long as it enjoyed working and running with its peers. But it had to be virtually non-distractable while in the harness, resisting all temptation to veer from its course or chase wild animals on the trail.

A good lead dog possessed the uncanny ability to sense hidden dangers, such as thin ice or water currents lying beneath crusted snow. The leader had to be able to find and follow a weak trail, despite blizzard conditions and many layers of fresh snow. Even when the driver had lost all sense of direction, the lead dog had to persevere. The fate of an entire team, sled, and driver could depend on the lead dog's unfailing dedication to its job.

Really good lead dogs came along infrequently, and sometimes drivers looked for them through many generations of dogs.

# 4 _____Sled Dogs
# Through the Years

*Through Mists of Time*

The Arctic peoples had many different religious beliefs about their dogs. Some Northern tribes thought that dogs guarded the gates to paradise. Often they sacrificed dogs to keep peace with their gods.

Eskimos believed that Indians and Europeans were descended from dogs, that a woman at the beginning of time had ten children who were fathered by a dog. Five of these children became Indians, while the other five set off on a raft, eventually to become Europeans.

It was common among some Eskimo tribes to allow dogs to help themselves to food at burial feasts. Tribal members felt that, by keeping the spirits happy, a dead person would have an easier time attaining paradise. Adam Brand, an early explorer, recorded this practice in 1698.

*Old print shows Lapp home. Note the dog.*

Lapp women offered dogs as sacrifices to the goddesses of childbirth. They hoped that by doing this they would have an easy delivery and a healthy baby. An historian visiting the Samoyed peoples in 1779 discovered that the tribesmen swore oaths on the blood of dogs. It was with the coming of missionaries bringing Christianity that many of these ceremonies disappeared.

*Old print of Mr. West, English missionary, visiting Indians in Canada. Note how details of harness and sled differ from the norm.*

*Early Jobs for Dogs*

Hauling sleds, herding, and hunting were not the only kinds of work performed by Arctic dogs. During the summer months, or in rough, mountainous terrain where sledging was impossible, dogs often were used as pack animals. Equally loaded cargo pouches were strapped on either side of the canines.

*Dog pulling travois*

Nomadic Arctic owners employed their dogs to pull a travois similar in design to that used by the Plains Indians of North America. It consisted of a platform supported by two long trailing poles. The forward ends of the poles were harnessed to the dog's back.

Of course, once the ancients learned to use dogs for hauling and the wheel was invented, dogs of every breed, in every corner of the world, were hitched to carts. Dog carts were used for transporting everything from soup to nuts. In Belgium, dogs pulled carts for daily milk deliveries, while mail still was being delivered by dog cart in Idaho as late as 1947!

*Raven, a lead dog, is an Alaskan Husky. Note the barrel kennels.*

### Into Today's World

It is said that the more modern employment of sled dogs dates back to 1873 when the Royal Canadian Mounted Police began using the dog team to "get their man." At that time, thousands of treasure seekers, lured by the thought of gold, were rushing frantically to the gold fields. To maintain law and order, the Mounties needed a fast way to cover the territories. Eventually, the Mounties came to favor the Mackenzie River strain of the so-called "Husky"—a strain composed of part Eskimo dog and part wolf, with mixes of Labrador Retriever, Newfoundland, and St. Bernard. It should be noted that "Husky" is a corruption of the Algonquin Indian word for Eskimo, *esky*. It is used incorrectly to refer to many dogs of the sled dog type but is applied by the AKC only to the Siberian Husky at this time.

It was not long before United States marshals also began using dog teams to bring justice to the gold mines. In addition, supplies had to be brought in to the mining camps and

ALASKA MALAMUTES, NOME.

— LOMEN BROS. NOME

*Working dogs of the gold fields photographed in 1906*

the gold brought out. Sled dog teams were kept busy for many years in these occupations.

*Polar Dogs*

At the same time the race for gold was going on, so were other races to the North and South poles. The earliest polar explorers make no mention of sled dogs in their records. Searching for a shortcut to the Orient, they relied on man-power to pull their heavily laden sledges on the early Arctic trips. It wasn't until the 1820's that dog-powered sledge travel was used on an Arctic exploration. Sir William Parry learned the techniques of sledging from the Eskimos and is credited with revolutionizing Arctic travel.

By the 1890's more Arctic explorers were using dogs. Fridtjof Nansen, who was forced to turn back only 224 miles from the North Pole, had designed a sled that worked so well almost every other Arctic or Antarctic explorer used it. It was made completely of wood and lashed with rawhide. Unfortunately, all of Nansen's dogs either died or were killed along the way. As a matter of fact, during almost every polar exploration, many dogs met the same fate. However, these dogs could be used to feed the other dogs or the men so that their deaths weren't a complete waste.

Sir Robert Edwin Peary, who also learned dog sledging directly from the Eskimos, in 1909 was the first man to reach the North Pole. His method for using both men and dogs was unique. He rotated teams and crews to forge ahead and blaze a trail. Frank Wilbert Stokes, an artist who traveled with Peary in this successful attempt, depicted the sledges being pulled by dogs harnessed in the fan formation. Peary

*A Nansen-type sled pictured during World War II*

had no problem returning from the Pole—he simply followed the urine stains his forty dogs had left on the way there.

While the world's attention was riveted on the race for the North Pole, other explorers were showing an interest in Antarctica and the South Pole. A painting of the expedition led by Lieutenant Charles Wilkes in 1840 shows his ship off the Antarctic coast with a shore party, including one large dog, on the ice. Just before the turn of the century, Carsten Borchgrevink, a Norwegian teacher turned explorer, took ninety Siberian dogs to Antarctica. Seventy-five of them became the first dogs to be used for Antarctic sledging.

Once the North Pole was reached officially, the race for the South Pole began in earnest. During the first two decades of the twentieth century, many attempts to reach the pole

*Old print shows members of Charles Wilkes' expedition, plus a very large dog, on the Antarctic continent, 1840.*

*Robert Scott preferred to depend on ponies for power across such Antarctic terrain as this being crossed by modern sled dog team.*

were made. Sir Robert Falcon Scott used sled dogs on his first try, 1901–1902. Unfortunately, Scott's dogs became ill. Their food, dried Norwegian stock fish, had spoiled on the trip through the tropics. When the expedition reached the colder climate it then froze, hiding the bad odor of spoiled food. When the dogs, already malnourished and run down, were given the fish, they became ill with vomiting and dysentery. There was no other food available to give them, and they got so weak they could barely pull. Scott, who was accompanied on this expedition by Ernest Shackleton, had to turn back only 238 miles from the pole, the closest anyone had ever come to it.

Scott had started this trip already prejudiced against dogs. He felt, along with many others, that using dogs was demeaning to the British ideas of manhood. Because he didn't want to use dogs, he didn't bother to learn much about how to care for or use them properly. Not understanding their physical makeup, he tried to force the dogs into his working patterns, never realizing that they did better in their own way.

Scott deplored the sled dog's love of fighting. He was shocked at their habit of eating their own excrement. All these dislikes, plus the fact that, through no fault of their own, the dogs had let Scott down, caused him to develop a distrust of them. This contributed to Scott's eventual downfall.

In 1907, Ernest Shackleton led his own expedition to Antarctica and attempted to reach the pole using Manchurian ponies for power. He calculated that one pony could pull twelve hundred pounds about twenty to thirty miles a day. Based on these figures, he took along only nine dogs and one motor car to help the ponies out. What he did not figure on was that the loss of one pony would be far more serious in terms of motive power than the loss of one dog. Although they got to within about one hundred miles of the pole, Shackleton and his men were forced to turn back. All the ponies either had died or been killed to feed the men.

Scott didn't learn from Shackleton's mistakes. Despite the fact that ponies were obviously not suited to Antarctic travel, Scott prepared for another attempt on the pole using ponies, tracked motor vehicles, man-hauling power, and thirty-three dogs, Siberians except for two that were Eskimos. Their driver, Demetri Gerof, was hired to go on the expedition with them.

The ponies worked as hard for Scott as their predecessors had for Shackleton. However, there was nothing they could do about the fact that their coats were just too thin for such frigid temperatures or that their feet were not suited to the ground they had to cover. Their little hooves caused them either to sink belly deep in soft snow or to slip and fall on the hard ice. The ponies suffered from hunger, and when one of their numbers died the others didn't benefit from its death because ponies are not carnivorous.

This last and fatal attempt of Scott's unintentionally turned out to be a race against Roald Amundsen of Norway.

*Historic photo of Amundsen's sled dogs and sled at the South Pole, with Oscar Wisting. Note dogs' size, massive heads, thick coats.*

Amundsen, who had learned about sledging on previous trips in the Arctic, understood canines. He worked his dogs the way they liked to be worked—a succession of sprints with frequent rests. When Amundsen tried to hitch his dogs in a pair by pair formation, they were clearly unhappy. Wisely he rehitched them in the fan formation, and they worked willingly. Using dogs, Amundsen reached the South Pole in December of 1911. Scott, after sending his dogs back to base because he did not think they could handle the terrain of the Beardmore Glacier, reached the pole in early 1912. All the ponies were sacrificed along the way to provide food for the rest of the expedition. Not only did the ponies fail to reach the pole but also Scott and his four companions of the polar party lost their lives on the return trip.

Later explorers, such as Admiral Richard Byrd in the late 1920's and the men who worked in 1957–58 during the International Geophysical Year, or IGY, used sled dogs with good results. In fact, except for Scott and Shackleton, every expedition that used sled dogs left testimonials to their usefulness, courage, stamina, and powers of endurance.

*Getting the Serum to Nome*

Sled dogs once again performed valiantly at the other end of the world when, in January of 1925, the city of Nome, Alaska, was stricken with an epidemic of diphtheria. The city's supply of antitoxin was quickly depleted, and the nearest source of the vital serum lay 955 miles away, in the city of Anchorage.

Nome was very near the sea, but the sea was frozen solid, rendering ships useless. Alaska's only two planes, having been dismantled for the winter, sat idle in Fairbanks, and the

*Leonhard Seppala pictured with team of his Siberian Huskies, 1916*

nearest ready-to-fly plane was in Seattle. Severe blizzard conditions, coupled with the great distance, made the trip by air too hazardous to risk.

Fortunately, it was possible to ship the medicine north from Anchorage to Nenana via railroad, a distance of almost 300 miles. Upon reaching Nenana, however, the serum still had to pass through 658 miles of treacherous terrain before reaching Nome. There was just one way to rush the life-or-death serum from Nenana to Nome: by relay teams of sled dogs.

By wire and wireless, the decision was made, the appeal for teams went out, the plans were laid. The precious serum was carried north by train, and on January 27, after a careful selection of dog teams and drivers, the race against time began at the Nenana Railroad Station. The Nenana-Nome route was a grueling one, even in fair weather. U.S. mail teams usually took twenty-five days to make the trek, but the people of Nome did not have that kind of time. The world

47

*Leonhard Seppala's Siberian Huskies photographed in their summer quarters, Cape Horn, Alaska*

waited anxiously as the fate of an entire city fell upon the heaving shoulders of sled dogs.

As teams of dogs raced northward from Nenana, Leonhard Seppala started driving a team of twenty Siberian Huskies southward from Nome to meet the serum. Seppala left twelve of the dogs at various villages along the way, to be used as fresh replacements on his return trip. When he passed Solomon, where the telephone line ended, he was out of communication with the world.

Toward the end of the fourth day, after traveling close to two hundred miles, Seppala and his team of eight Siberians met up with the serum supply, by then on its fifteenth relay team. Seppala had not expected to meet the serum so soon, but the northbound schedule had been stepped up. Because the deadly epidemic had reached massive proportions, the relays were covering shorter distances with fresh dogs. The teams were running night and day to speed the serum to Nome.

When he intercepted the serum, Seppala and his team, led by the veteran trail dog Togo, had already driven forty-two miles in one day through blizzard conditions, with temperatures holding steady at thirty degrees below zero. Nevertheless, Seppala transferred the package of serum to his sled, turned around, and started to retrace his route.

The worst stretch of the trip lay directly before him: the ice of Norton Sound, from Isaacs Point to Shaktoolik. As night approached, the wind grew savage, greatly increasing the danger of ice breaking away and floating off into the

*A note on this April, 1906, photograph describes it as a dog team ride on the Bering Sea, Nome. Looking at the ice, one can only imagine the conditions Seppala and Togo and the team met when crossing Norton Sound in the blizzard.*

Bering Sea. On the fifth day, Seppala varied his trail slightly, driving the team closer to shore. Later he realized that his icy trail of the previous day had already broken away and drifted out to sea.

Seppala and Togo drove the longest distance by far: 340 miles in all. No other team covered more than 53 miles. The distance weighed heavily upon Togo. Left permanently lame by the run, the old dog never made another long trip.

The final leg of the journey—including the famed reentry into Nome at 5:30 A.M. on February 2, 1925—was made by Gunnar Kasson and his team, under the leadership of Balto, a half-wolf sled dog. To the horror of many Alaskans, U.S. reporters gave the greatest publicity to Balto, endowing him with Togo's mileage record and billing Balto, rather than Togo, as "the greatest racing leader in Alaska."

The life-giving journey from Nenana to Nome was covered by dog teams over a period of five and a half days. To commemorate the sled dogs' diligent struggle in this race for life, a statue of Balto was erected in New York City's Central Park. The inscription on the statue reads:

Dedicated to the indomitable spirit of the sled dogs
that relayed antitoxin six-hundred miles over rough
ice, across treacherous waters, through Arctic
blizzards, from Nenana to the relief of stricken Nome
in the Winter of 1925.

Endurance     Fidelity     Intelligence

*Dogs in War*

Dogs have a long history of serving men in war. It is recorded that in 700 B.C., when man fought against man and horse against horse, so did "dog against dog." Celtic,

Roman, and Persian armies unleashed dogs and sent them into enemy lines to cause confusion. The Gauls gave coats of chain mail to dogs as protective armor, and added spiked collars to wound the legs of enemy horses during a cavalry charge.

Throughout man's almost constant warfare, dogs have served as guards, sentries, and messengers. Sled dog breeds are credited with work in mountainous areas during World War I. Eskimo dogs were cited for making high grades at the War Dog School in England. Of 150 dogs assembled in America to be sent overseas, several were Malamutes with good hauling records.

Siberian Huskies and Malamutes were recruited for sledging during World War II, and teams of sled dogs were used by the U.S. Army's Arctic Search and Rescue Unit of the Air Transport Command. When a plane crashed in terrain too rough for other planes to land, dogs, sleds, drivers, and equipment were parachuted into the region. Although initially frightened by the fall, the dogs quickly regained composure and were able to work together effectively.

*Sled dogs in freight harness pull a toboggan-type sled during World War II at a war dog training center.*

CHATTANOOGA HAMILTON CO.
BICENTENNIAL LIBRARY

*Seventeen-dog team pulling 1500 pounds up a 41% grade in Newfound-
land during World War II. Men and dogs, sent to establish a search and
rescue unit, were assigned the task of freighting a complete radio station
to the top of a mountain for the Signal Corps.*

Following Nazi Germany's breakthrough at the Battle of the Bulge in December of 1944, teams of sled dogs were used to locate wounded soldiers and transport them to safety behind Allied lines. The Air Force even employed sled dogs to search for hydrogen bombs lost in a plane accident over Greenland some years later.

Sled dogs have been used individually in war as guard dogs. One in particular—a part Siberian Husky, part Collie, part German Shepherd named Chips—served its unit well. On July 10, 1943, Chips landed in Sicily with the 3rd Infantry Division of General George Patton's 7th Army. The moment the soldiers hit the sandy beach, they were immobilized by machine-gun fire from a nearby hut. Suddenly Chips raced right for the hut. Amid much confusion and noise, the firing ceased. Seconds later, an Italian soldier came stumbling out with Chips grappling at his throat. Chips's handler called off the dog, fearing the man would be killed. Three other machine gunners within the hut were quick to surrender after seeing the ferocity of the American canine in combat.

Soon afterward, Chips was recommended for the Distinguished Service Cross. The commander of the Third Division agreed that Chips deserved recognition, but he was hesitant to bestow so high a medal upon a dog. The commander awarded Chips the Silver Star "for bravery in action against the enemy." The United States War Department revoked the award, however, feeling that Chips was "only a dog."

Although Chips's pride suffered little by this reverse decision, the outrage voiced by his fellow G.I.'s—the men whose lives he saved on that beach in Sicily—was boundless. They looked upon Chips as one of the war's most famous heroes.

# 5 _____ *Racing*

Since the beginning of time men have challenged each other to races. Who can say for sure when the first race between sled dog teams took place? Perhaps hundreds of years ago one Inuit said to another, "My team is better than yours." Such a challenge probably would have prompted a race to prove who indeed had the better team.

Records of organized sled dog racing, according to the central governing body of the sport, the International Sled Dog Racing Association, or ISDRA, started in 1908 with the first running of the All-Alaska Sweepstakes. This race covered 408 miles from Nome to Candle and back. It has been run ever since, except for breaks during both World Wars.

Opinions seem to differ concerning the beginnings of racing in the conterminous U.S.A. Some authorities say that

WINNERS FIRST ANNUAL ALL-ALASKA SWEEPSTAKES. NOME, ALASKA.

*Organized sled dog racing records started with this race in 1908, according to the International Sled Dog Racing Association.*

Arthur Walden, returning to his native New Hampshire from the Alaskan gold fields, was so thrilled about sled dog racing that he trained and raced a team of crossbreds. This led to the belief that the first organized race in the Lower 48 was held in the Tamworth, Wonalancet, and Chocura area of New Hampshire. Traditionally this race is still the first of every season. Other records state emphatically that the first

*A Wonalancet basket sled, photographed at an Army installation, during World War II. Note Quonset hut.*

race in the conterminous United States took place in 1917 in Ashton, Idaho.

One thing is certain—organized sled dog racing gained popularity in leaps and bounds. In 1924, the first American sled dog club was formed. Since then, clubs have sprung up all over the country. Today the ISDRA sanctions over a hundred races a year and lists members in forty-two states, nine Canadian provinces, and seven European countries.

Modern sled dog races seem to have evolved into two basic types—sprint and endurance. The sprint races are of short or mid length and the heats may span a few days. Many states, towns, and cities sponsor them. Whether endorsed by the ISDRA or by individual sled dog clubs, these races follow the same basic formats and are eagerly looked forward to by participants as well as spectators.

Sprint races are closed-course events over a set number of miles. The teams start and finish at the same place. Different-sized teams of three, five, seven, or an unlimited number of dogs participate in different events. Sprint races can be one, five, ten, sixteen, or more miles long. The teams leave the starting line at carefully timed intervals. Mass starts are rarely used today except in Canada.

The races are timed events and may be composed of more than one heat, or division. If for some reason one of the dogs can't compete in subsequent heats, a musher is allowed to leave that dog out of the team but cannot substitute another in its place. Numbers are drawn to determine starting positions. Everyone hopes that teams known for their slowness will pick the higher numbers. Slow teams in the lead positions force faster-moving, later-starting teams to go around them.

*Passing on the trail during a race*

To pass another team, a musher must shout "Trail!" The team ahead then pulls to the side of the trail, often stopping until the faster team passes. All this increases the chances of an accident.

During a race a driver has to balance around turns so the sled doesn't flip over. If there are any downhills, he must turn his heels in and drag them to slow the sled up so it doesn't run into the wheel, or near, dogs. The driver never sits on a sled during a race. He rides on the runners or pedals instead.

Other contests are popular events at the race meets. There are weight pulls, where the dogs have a number of chances to move a set of weights a given distance, and freight races, where the dogs travel shorter distances pulling a certain

*Their friendship cemented after a timid approach, this boy and young Siberian Husky may grow up to enter a Kid and Mutt race together.*

number of pounds. "Kid and Mutt" races, in which a child drives one dog of any breed or mix, are very popular.

The Iditarod Trail Race which began in Alaska in 1973 is the longest and perhaps the best known of the endurance races. In this race, teams of up to eighteen dogs travel over one thousand miles from Anchorage to Nome. The trail follows in part the old supply route to the gold camps of yesteryear. This race can take anywhere from ten days to four weeks. To make good time, the teams should cover one hundred miles a day. Drivers and dogs usually get no more than three to four hours of sleep per each twenty-four, but one 24-hour rest stop is mandatory during the race. Dogs and humans suffer from severe weather conditions, including below-zero temperatures and the ever-present threat of snowblindness. Veterinarians and volunteers man twenty-five checkpoints along the way. Dogs unfit to travel for any

*On the trail, the Alpo International Sled Dog Championship, 1982*

*Harris Dunlap, 1982 World Champion Sled Dog racer, with team of his own strain of Alaskan Huskies at Alpo International Sled Dog Championship*

reason can be left at these points. Food and supplies must be flown in to resting places along the trail. Nowadays, many women as well as men compete in this grueling race, as they do in sprint races.

There are other well-known races. In Laconia, New Hampshire, snow makers are used for the yearly race if there is not enough snow. Upstate New Yorkers anticipate the annual Alpo International Sled Dog Championship held in the Adirondacks. There are races at Ely, Minnesota, and Truckee, California. Since 1936, Anchorage, Alaska, has hosted the Anchorage Rendezvous World Sled Dog Race, or the Rondy, as it is sometimes called. Canada has many races, with the World Championship Dog Derby, held in The Pas, Manitoba, the longest and hardest.

Advocates of sled dog racing feel that the racing dogs are the cream of the animal athletes, out performing anything else with legs, even humans. The dogs have the ability to run at speeds of twenty or more miles per hour across snow and ice in below-freezing temperatures. Much attention is given to the health of these dogs, and trips to the vet are common.

Recent research has proved that nutrition does play an important part in the animals' ability to run. Special care is taken to provide the racing dogs with a balanced, fortified diet based on meat. This diet must be compact, digestible, and high in protein to maintain energy levels.

Racing dogs are not necessarily purebreds. While the well-known Arctic breeds are frequently used, it is not an

*Many people consider sled dogs to be the cream of animal athletes. These lead dogs were photographed at the 1983 annual sled dog races on Great Sacandaga Lake, Northville, New York.*

*Racing scenes: Dogs being fed on a tether line in falling snow;*

uncommon sight to see Coonhounds, Dalmatians, Retrievers, and even Airedales and Irish Setters competing. Dogs weighing only about fifty pounds and standing approximately twenty-four inches at the shoulders are the most popular for sprint racing. The heavier Malamutes and Samoyeds generally do well in the longer endurance or freight races. The dogs for these races must have deep chests with good lung capacity. Strong backs and tough, compact feet are also essential.

Many modern breeders have been crossbreeding, attempting to produce great racing strains. Many have developed their own lines of the Alaskan Husky and with them have won race after race. Fanciers of the Alaskan Husky keep close records and breed carefully. Some of the strains are accepted by the Alaskan Husky Club.

To be good racers, dogs must be willing and eager to

*Dogs on tether line wait to race. Note Coonhound, right center;*

run—to be so excited by running that they won't give up. The dogs must be able to take the pressures and stresses involved with training and racing. Dogs may run up to two thousand miles during training, then travel thousands of miles by truck to race many more miles. All this while remaining in tiptop condition.

Drivers look for dogs that are even tempered and gentle. The dogs can't allow crowds and excitement at a race to throw them off stride. A snapping dog is never allowed on a team. Neither is a dog that fights with the other dogs. There is relatively little sex discrimination on a racing team. Either males or females have the potential for becoming good racing dogs.

*Racing sleds rest on dog boxes on a truck bed.*

*Mushers don't use whips, as pictured in this old print. There is no physical contact between driver and team during a race.*

As noted, a good lead dog is vital to a team and is the only dog really trained to follow the voice commands of the musher. Therefore, the lead dog must have the respect and obedience of its teammates so they will follow him, or her. Imagine how far a team would get with the leader going in one direction and the rest of the team in another! All the dogs and the musher must work together toward the common goal: Winning.

The musher is as important as the dogs in winning a race. It is he who trains, commands, and controls his team. Praise rather than punishment is the preferred method of training. The musher must make training and racing fun so the dogs will continue to love to run. Treating the dogs with kindness produces the character traits mushers look for in their teams.

Contrary to the popular image, a musher does not shout frenzied commands at his dogs while flailing a long whip across their backs. If he carries a whip at all, it is short and used only to separate dogs in the event of a fight. The musher has no physical contact with his team during a race. Without reins, only his voice and his personality control the dogs.

After training his dogs to respond to specific verbal commands, the musher strictly adheres to this vocabulary. The fewer words and syllables per command, the better. To start his team, for example, he may call out "Let's go!" or "Hike!" or "Okay!" while his voice bursts with enthusiasm. The word "Mush!" is seldom used by experienced drivers. It lacks impact when shouted and is too soft sounding, and thus is impractical as a command to be used on the trail.

Since dogs are sensitive to sounds rather than to specific words, the musher's sparse vocabulary can be heightened by a vast range of vocal inflections. Often he will develop his own variations of standard commands to avoid confusion in racing and make sure his dogs don't respond to the commands of another driver.

Close communication between the musher and his dogs is essential at all times. Some drivers use whistles rather than words to guide their dogs. In situations where the lead dog cannot hear the musher's commands—due to bad weather, an unusually large number of dogs, or rough, steep trails—a musher may use a series of short jerks of the tug line to get the leader's attention.

The musher is largely responsible for the happiness and success of his team. He is alert to the danger signals of team driving and attempts to ward off major problems before they settle in. For example, booties of heavy cloth fastened to the dogs' feet prior to crossing rough snow or ice can avert torn and sore paws. The musher watches out for signs of exhaustion or injury among his dogs. It is the musher's job to keep the sled from running up on his team, an event sure to cause tangled lines and snarling dogs. If personality problems arise between teammates, the driver may try repositioning those

*A kiss from a Siberian Husky can be a child's reward for helping.*

particular dogs to achieve a more harmonious formation.

A good musher treats his dogs fairly and as individuals, yet never tolerates any sign of aggression. It is said in Alaska that veterinary bills are the only reward for the lenient musher. A good musher singles out a misbehaving dog, calling the animal by its name and carefully avoiding use of any words to which the entire team might respond.

The musher fills the vital role of maintaining order among a group of lively dogs that love to run. Above all else in dealing with his team, the musher must be consistent— consistent in his commands, his harnessing and unharnessing techniques, his expectations of the dogs, and his procedures for discipline and reward. Through consistency, the musher can best attain control and bypass chaos, enabling man and dog to strike a healthy balance of respect . . . and friendship.

Sled dog racing is very much a family affair. Everyone participates. Dogs must be fed and cared for and cleaned up after every day. Children in a family are often assigned some

*"Are you ready?"*        *"Let's go!"*

LEFT: *Children help puppies get used to humans.* RIGHT: *These 9-month-old puppies, bred to race at Go Kennel, are a mix of Siberian Husky, Borzoi, Great Dane, Greyhound, and Blue-tick Coonhound.*

of these chores. Dogs also must be bred, whelped, raised, and trained. The children, by playing with the puppies, get them accustomed to being around humans.

Training goes on year round unless the weather is too hot. Dehydration is a problem with dogs during very hot weather because of a limited ability to sweat, so training is kept to a minimum then. When the weather is cool but there is no snow, the dogs are harnessed to a light three-wheeled training cart, or gig.

As soon as they are old enough, at about three months,

puppies are allowed to run with the team. The next step is to harness them with seasoned veterans. The puppies learn from the older dogs and hopefully catch some of the racing enthusiasm that is so necessary to win. The pups must learn to get used to the pulling and tugging of their lines as well as how not to get the lines tangled. All the while they are learning, the young dogs are carefully watched for leadership abilities.

Many "mushing families" spend up to three winter months a year following the racing circuit. Parents feel that taking their children with them and keeping the family unit whole is important. Children keep up with their school assignments through special arrangements worked out with the schools.

The equipment used for sled dog racing is pretty much the same today as it was in the beginning. Only some of the materials have changed. Racing sleds have evolved from the Alaskan freight sleds. They are built for speed, durability, and braking power. An average racing sled is about eight feet long and weighs less than forty pounds. The sleds are always made of wood such as ash, birch, or hickory that has been

*Diagram of a racing sled*

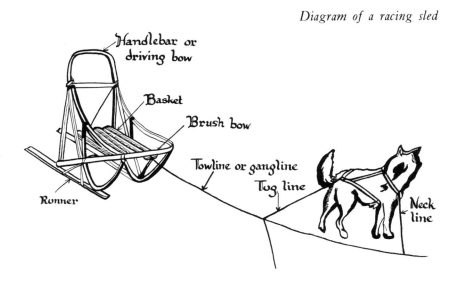

*The joy of riding behind a great team of dogs . . .*

steam bent. They are lashed together mostly with nylon, although rawhide is still used sometimes. There is a bow called the brush bow at the front of the sled as a bumper against collision. The runners, depending on weather conditions, are covered for protection with steel or plastic strips instead of being coated with ice or mud as in the old days.

The gang hitch is the most popular racing hitch. This method allows for either one or two lead dogs on a team. Racing sleds must carry dog bags. If a dog is unable to continue the race because it is tired or injured, it must be zipped inside this bag and carried on the sled for the remainder of the race.

It is interesting and thrilling to watch a sled dog race. As the anxious dogs are lined up in the starting chute, most are straining against their harnesses and whining. Many, despite being held by handlers, still manage to leap up and down in their excitement.

As the loudspeaker blares "Five—four—three—two—one. Let them go!" you can hear the musher calling to his team, "Are you ready, boys? Are you ready?" The dogs' frenzy visibly heightens. At the signal, the handlers release the dogs, which surge forward. The musher yells, "All right, boys, let's go!" or something similar, as he or she runs behind the sled, pushing it off to a good start. As the team races away, you still can hear the voice of the driver urging the dogs on. By now the musher probably is either astride the runners or pedaling.

While awaiting the return of the first teams, you may watch others still starting out, depending on the length of the race. The first team out is not necessarily the first one back.

Watching the teams return is a moving sight. Despite their obvious tiredness, most of the dogs are still eager and willing to run. At this point the driver may again be pedaling, or perhaps crouching down on the runners behind the sled to lower wind resistance. Rarely has the musher stopped his endless encouragement of his team. Often at the end of a race you will see the musher hugging his dogs one by one, starting with the lead dog and going right down the line. The dogs really like this and respond enthusiastically.

Although few races offer big prizes, more and more people are taking up the sport. That it is an expensive sport is undeniable. Often the prize monies don't even cover expenses. However, many mushers obviously feel that the joy of riding behind a team of dogs more than compensates for the lack of financial rewards. Dog people have long been noted for such devotion to their fancy.

Sled dog races are becoming a popular spectator sport as well. The excitement, the noise and bustle, and the delight of watching the dogs are attracting more and more spectators every year. There is no admission charge for a sled dog race. Sometimes, the best things in life are free.

*Dog tired!*

# 6 _The Future_

Today's world is basically an automated one with machines replacing men and animals in the work field. In the Northern regions where once the quiet was broken only by the creak of sleds over ice, the occasional commands of the musher, or the excited yipping of the dogs, it is now far more common to hear the raucous sputter of snowmobiles, tractors, or other motorized vehicles. However, recent research shows that there is a tendency, albeit a slight one, to return to the sled dog teams as a form of transportation. This is especially true in a few Inuit outposts on Baffin Island in the north, and in New Zealand, Australia, and British settlements on Antarctica.

In these places, people feel that dogs are more dependable than machines. Dogs can go where tractors or snowmobiles can't, and they rarely break down. If lost in the snow or ice, dogs will always find their way back by using their keen sense of smell. What machine can do that? Also, the dogs provide companionship through the long winter months.

Probably the most important reason for this new trend is economic. Machines and parts are expensive. So are gas and oil. And supplies are usually far away. The cost of shipping supplies to remote regions, furthermore, is prohibitive.

Commercial food for dogs, even with the added cost of transportation, has to be less expensive than gasoline. Further, it is possible to catch fresh food from the sea for a team.

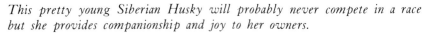

*This pretty young Siberian Husky will probably never compete in a race but she provides companionship and joy to her owners.*

*Dogs can always sniff their way back if they get lost on the trail. This driver has provided booties to help his team go in snow.*

*Alaskan Malamute, popular in the show ring as well as on the trail*

You can't go out and catch a few gallons of gas for machines!
Another economic plus for the dogs is that they can reproduce themselves at little or no cost. Machines don't have that
ability!

Then, perhaps the ultimate and practical reason for using
dogs over snowmobiles, as given by an old Inuit, is that, if
you are starved, "You can't eat your snowmobile." Many an
explorer has had to make such a grim decision about his dogs
to save his own life.

Purebred Malamutes, Samoyeds, and Siberian Huskies are becoming increasingly popular in the show ring. Spectators as well as participants at dog shows thrill to the sight of the magnificent beasts as they are gaited, or moved, around the ring by their handlers. Watching them, it is easy to visualize long lines of the ancestors of these breeds—perhaps of these very dogs—mushing across polar wastes in their centuries of service to man.

*Champion Kazakh's Albert of Barbicon, product of the centuries*

# Glossary

*All right! Hike! Let's go! Okay!* Interchangeable terms used to start teams of dogs. Others are *Get up! Go ahead! Hup!*

*American Kennel Club.* Organization in the U.S.A. devoted to the advancement of purebred dogs.

*At the alert.* Describes position of dog's body when attentive.

*Basket.* Body of sled used for carrying people or goods.

*Brake.* Heavy metal fork. When its prongs are forced into the snow, it stops a sled.

*Breed.* A genetic strain, usually of a domestic animal, having the same recognizable inherited characteristics.

*Brush bow.* Bumper at front of sled.

*Canadian Kennel Club.* Organization in Canada devoted to the advancement of purebred dogs.

*Conterminous.* Having a common boundary; here the first forty-eight of the United States.

*Crossbred.* Animal produced by mixing breeds within a species.

*Crossbreeding.* Mating different breeds or varieties within a species.

*Dehydration.* Excessive loss of water from body. Can cause death.

*Diphtheria.* An acute contagious disease.

*Dog bag.* Bag into which dog unable to complete a race is zipped and carried on sled.

*Dog box.* Box divided into sections and mounted on a truck.

*Draft animal.* One that draws a load.

*Driving bow* or *Handlebar.* Curved bar at rear of sled to which driver holds.

*Endurance race.* Long, demanding race.

*Fancy.* That which pleases; here the breeding of animals to develop excellence.

*Fan hitch.* Connects all the dogs to a sled at one point.

*Freight race.* Dog must pull a specified number of pounds a short distance.

*Gaited.* Animal being moved in specified way.

*Gang hitch.* Connects dogs in pairs to the central gangline.

*Gangline* or *Towline.* Center line in harnessing dogs to sled.

*Handlebar. See Driving bow.*

*Harness.* The gear, other than a yoke, used by a draft animal to pull a vehicle; an arrangement of straps.

*Heat.* A single course or a division of a race.

*Hitch.* Way of connecting a draft animal to its load.

*Kid and Mutt race.* A child drives one dog in this type of race.

*Lead dog.* First dog on gangline. Two dogs can be used in a double lead.

*Linebreeding.* Breeding within a particular line of descent to reproduce certain desirable characteristics.

*Lines.* Cable, cord, rawhide, rope, string, or wire used to harness dogs to sled.

*Lower 48.* The first forty-eight of the United States.

*Man-hauling.* Men pulling sleds or sledges.

*Mush!* Term infrequently used to start a team.

*Musher.* Driver of a team of sled dogs.

*Neck line.* Light line hooking dog's collar to gangline.

*Pedaling* or *Pumping.* Pushing with one foot while other foot remains on runner.

*Pedigree.* The recorded lineage of a purebred animal.

*Point dogs.* Dogs on gangline immediately behind lead dog.

*Pumping. See Pedaling.*

*Purebred.* Animal with a recorded lineage within a breed for many generations.

*Riding the runners.* Musher standing on runners.

*Runners.* Strips on which a sled slides. Today they may be covered with steel or plastic; formerly they were often covered with frozen mud for smoothness.

*Sled/Sledge.* Interchangeable terms for a vehicle mounted on low runners and pulled over snow and ice.

*Snow hook.* Hook attached by a line to sled and used to stake out a team.

*Sprint race.* A race of short duration.

*Standard.* A degree or level of requirement or attainment.

*Swing dogs.* All dogs on gangline between point and wheel dogs.

*Tandem hitch.* Connects dogs singly or alternately along the gangline or towline.

*Towline. See Gangline.*

*Trail!* Demand for right of way on a trail.

*Tug line.* Line fastening dog harness to the gangline.

*Tundra.* Treeless plains of the Arctic.

*Weight pull.* Contest in which a dog is given a number of chances to move a set of weights a certain distance.

*Wheel dogs.* Dogs on gangline closest to sled.

*Whelp.* To give birth to young.

# Index